Our Invisible Supply: How to Obtain

Francis Larimer Warner

Copyright © 2012

All rights reserved. No part of this publication may be reproduced or transmitted for commercial purposes, except for brief quotation in printed reviews, without written permission of the publisher.

Printed in the United States of America

ISBN: 1481024728
ISBN-13: 978-1481024723

PREFACE

As an introduction to this little book, and explanatory of its purpose, I print immediately following this preface, three very appreciative letters from students. These, selected from many more, first suggested to me the idea of compiling a few of my letters to students in book form, since they seem to have proven helpful, and humanity's problems are about alike the world over. In this way their field of usefulness will be enlarged, and no one has the right to withhold a helping hand or word when possible to give.

In the arrangement of the book, I have followed my letters by three short articles which emphasize my individual teaching in the matter of calling into action the Law of Supply, and which when printed in the columns of one of our magazines brought to me so many letters of inquiry and appeal, as to show that many were seeking for the truth which I had demonstrated. To help others who have like problems, these articles are reprinted here,—the third ("An Elucidation") to prevent any misconception or misapplication of my methods of demonstrating the Law of Supply.

        Frances Larimer Warner. Philip, South Dakota.

CONTENTS

THREE LETTERS FROM STUDENTS OF FRANCES LARIMER WARNER...1

Letter One..5

Letter Two 8

Letter Three..12

Letter Four..15

Letter Five...19

Letter Six...22

Letter Seven 26

Letter Eight...30

Letter NIne 34

Letter Ten 37

Letter Eleven..40

Letter Twelve 43

Letter ThirTEEN..47

Letter Fourteen 50

Letter FIFteen..53

Letter Sixteen...57

Letter SevenTeen...60

Letter Eighteen..64

Letter Nineteen 68

"THE WORD WAS GOD."	71
"THE INVISIBLE RESOURCE."	73
AN ELUCIDATION	76
TESTIMONIAL	78

THREE LETTERS FROM STUDENTS OF FRANCES LARIMER WARNER

—printed here as an example of the needs which exist all about us, and which it is the object of this book to teach us how to satisfy, through the Law of Supply.

My Dear Lover of Souls:

YOU really knew what I needed, for your letter has gone to the spot and has really done me more good than most things that have come into my pathway

for years. "To consecrate yourself an empty vessel to the one intelligence and source of supply that knows no limitation at all." All right. Let me tell you a little demonstrating I did the week I wrote you. I held the thought that God was my supply. I sent down town by a friend for a little brown teapot; when I came home in the afternoon rather tired— ought one to say so?—I had our cook make me a cup of tea. On uncovering the teapot I found inside the cover a delicious stick of almond brittle. A night or two afterwards brought me a delicious treat of ice cream delivered at the door. These are exceedingly material items, aren't they?

I am possessed of a longing for a home—oh, such a home, with a library. And in the library is a grate fire of wood; before the grate fire are two people; I know them. Well, I picked up the Literary Digest, Monday, and there pictured on the first page, or rather cover, was a roaring fire of wood, no paltry or artificial gas.

Then today I happened on the lines of Evangeline about Basil going to their home and Gabriel bidding him welcome to the hearth, while above me as I write is my "Hanging of the Crane." What shall I do?

Build my fire, then erect my home around it? Is the law beginning to work a bit? You say "This attractive force is an intelligence, and it brings us in touch with the ways and means." I guess that is one thing that has been the trouble with me. I have been doing some graduate work at Columbia, and came here with the determination to try to gain some recognition in a literary way by starting out with research articles. I have worked at the Peabody library quite a bit this fall but have had to dog myself to it. Have felt purely creative work was mine, something seemed to tell me so. So I waited. I have never sent anything for publication; in fact, have never finished anything in right shape, but am always possessed with the longing, the desire, the feeling I can. Is there a law that governs creative work? Oh, this must be a beautiful life to live when one thoroughly grasps the whole significance, when one can, as you say you do, really feel one's self an instrument in the hands of God, the Good, one to whom all good may come, from whom all good may flow. Is it really and truly so, no myth, no fake? I do not mean to ask you—to doubt—because there is that quality in your letter which makes for Truth; I mean rather to exclaim at the wonder of it. I found a dainty little handkerchief down town for you today, I thought perhaps you would not have the same opportunity to find pretty things in Dakota. With sincerest thanks for your letter,

Your appreciating,
M.S. F.

Dear Friend:

I WRITE you with a heart full of gratitude for your most helpful and encouraging letter. Many of the statements were so forceful and at the same time so simple and convincing that it "struck home" better than anything I have read along this line before. Even while the actual demonstration has not appeared in the visible, I do believe it exists at this moment in the invisible and real substance, and will manifest itself in the outer world some tune. The statement that seemed to appeal to me most, perhaps, was that money (and I also apply it to my health) is but the symbol of the exhaustless fountain of all supply and harmony in the real substance; and if held with a taut rein, we withhold the substance; so I am trying to let go the rein and let in the overflow of all that I need and desire. There seems to be one question that perplexes me just along this line, or perhaps should say about this matter of supply. The matter of physical healing I can comprehend, as the body is here, a tangible presence; but it seems that while the infinite supply is inexhaustible, we ourselves have to make a certain amount of effort to bring about results. For instance, by simply sitting down and visualizing the desire for a million dollars, (to take an extreme case), would you get it? I should think not, unless one had the requisite amount of faith, ability and work to bring about the result. You told me about visualizing the home you desired and actually bringing about the desired condition. I like the idea immensely, only cannot quite reconcile it with what I have just said. If you would be so good as to again explain it to me I should be very grateful. I am anxious to learn and to grow, that I may be the means sometime of giving light and help to others. Again, do you think one is selfish in desiring material things and endeavoring to demonstrate their possession in this way? To bring a commonsense view to the case, (while to be sure the ideal view is to work selflessly,) at the stage in evolution of the majority of mortals and I know in my own case, I do require certain necessities and desire certain luxuries or simple pleasures and am not ashamed to confess it, while at the same time that to which I would like to devote my life most of all would be active work along these New Thought lines. I love the teachings, the world needs them, and I would like to do my share in giving them out. Have made a few typewritten copies of your good letter which I am sending to you together with the original, thinking possibly you may find it convenient to have it in typewritten form for future reference. Also enclose one dollar by way of a small offering of appreciation of your kindness in giving me the suggestions that you have. Thanking you again for the same, I am,

Lovingly yours,

J. M. E.

Dear Friend:

I FEEL I cannot half express my appreciation for your goodness and dearness in giving me so much of your attention, and the little offering I enclose is very far from being anything like adequate for the value received, but is all my present circumstances allow. When I begin to demonstrate improved conditions, it will be my first pleasure to express more fully the gratitude in my heart. Your letter was so exactly what I have longed for, the testimony of one who has proved step by step these beautiful theories which seem to our matter-clouded senses intangible, almost unattainable ideals. I felt after reading your article, as many did—could that be for me? And now your dear letter comes, with its heart-warming assurances that it is within my power to attain. You are very good, indeed, to so freely give the stranger knocking at your gates, the golden key which has unlocked for you such treasures after years of searching; and my heart thrills with gratitude and wonder each time I think such chance has come to me. For your words are vital, and I cannot help feeling assured that I have now the clue, and it rests with me to overcome finally. I have been much troubled in all my efforts hitherto by two things; first, inability to concentrate; and, second, and perhaps for that reason, that I have failed to make live and actual my conception of God and His abiding place within me and so my "treatments" became mere words to me, for all my earnest desire. But I think your method of imagery, if I understand aright, is not dependent on the use of formulas, or at least one comes to use one's own words. Professor Northrup, in his article in January, says; "Put yourself in touch with God" when asking anything, and that is where I stick—I don't realize any connection. For meditation I seem to have very little time, as my evenings are almost always subject to interruption, and my days spent at business. I shall try to follow your directions during my hour's ride to and from the city, and at all other times when I can happen to catch myself in the custom paths of limitation thought. There is another thought that bothers also, and that is; How do we know that "Desire is the thing itself," or that God is more anxious for us to have than we are to receive? This is one of my worst stumbling blocks, so long do the effects of orthodox teachings cling to one—that our afflictions are sent to chasten us, and that certain disagreeable conditions we are placed in, are for our good, the strengthening of our characters, etc., no matter how useless and trying they seem to us. You see I am taking advantage of your generous invitation to ask any questions. If I could only tell you how much I appreciate your giving me this glorious hope, and the time and trouble you have taken to make the way clear, which you surely did! It is proof of the existence of that all too rare thing, Christ-Christianity, and I am so glad, so glad I wrote you. Be sure my love and grateful thoughts will attend you, and your letter I shall keep by me to read and reread and practice. Thanking you from my heart, I am a loving 'friend,

F. E. B.

LETTER ONE

A lesson in proving the Law of Supply

Dear Friend:

YOU say the law of supply is one of the laws you desire to learn. What you really mean is that you desire to *prove* the one great Law as your supply. Well, I gave you an opportunity to prove it in my last letter and you refused to see. Why is it so hard to comprehend, when it is so simple? You cannot expect a flow of oil or increase of meal until you *begin to use;* you cannot pour water from a pitcher until you take the pitcher in hand and begin to pour. Herein is one of the mighty occult truths I promised to give when you had complied with my terms. I do not need your money, but I *do* need *your faith in me* in order to be of assistance to you, and as you are a strong personality I felt the current of doubt and distrust that was sent out with your letter, and got, through telepathy, the very thought sent out with it. That which comes to me from this work I use in spreading Truth. You have first to learn the very first principles of faith before you can possibly demonstrate great or "many things." Jesus would or could not help his own people because of *their* unbelief and never helped any one without abundant proof of their faith in him. We all draw to us, through the law of attraction, all the good and all the error that we experience. When I learned this to be infallible, I gloried in spending my last dime for a luxury. Why? Because I would not allow myself to believe that I needed it for a necessity, since I am heir to all wealth. The first time I did this, I went home and found a letter with money enclosed as payment for something purchased of me some time before. *"Before you call, I will answer,"* and every time I proved this Law I received full measure pressed down and running over.

Money is not wealth, but the symbol only of inexhaustible wealth that will never begin to flow for us until we begin to prove, and when we have proven, stand fast in the faith. For *"let not him that wavereth, expect anything of the Law,"* says Paul. As long as we limit and fear to use the symbol of wealth, how can the real substance flow? For just as surely as we pinch and hold the symbol, just so surely do we hold the flow of the unseen (though not invisible) supply, which explains the saying that *"without faith it is impossible to please God,"* because Good cannot flow as supply when we ourselves are holding it back with a taut rein. Let us cease insulting our Good by hugging our rags and tatters of doubt and fear so closely about us, and begin to act and live as becomes our royal estate. We have no respect for the miser who clothes himself in rags and lives on a crust. How do many of us differ from him?

This letter is not just what you expected, but was needful to your present stage of progress or the Spirit would not have given it, since I am only a channel for truth. *"The Father within me doeth the works."* What you really desire is the abundant supply not limited to "one thousand dollars," and to become a channel for good to the world through articles, perhaps in the form of short stories. Oh, dear heart! all you need to insure the greatest success is to consecrate yourself an empty vessel to the one intelligence and source of supply that knows no limitation at all. I like to image myself as empty of self and the Good flowing through me to those who come to me for Truth, and as surely as you practice this attitude towards Spirit will you become more and more a fitting instrument for all good to others. Make yourself receptive, in other words, to the highest, and the ideals you have formed will soon give place to those most exalted. Henry Wood says that ideals have an attractive force and I know he is right and that we have to give no thought to the ways and means, as this attractive force is also an intelligence, and *it* brings us in touch with ways and means.

When I hear from you again, will continue this topic for my next letter. Sincerely hoping that you will gain some idea from this as to how to set the Law in motion as your supply and all other good, I am,

Very cordially yours,
FRANCES LARIMER WARNER.

"Do not require a description of the countries towards which you sail. The description does not describe them to you, and tomorrow you arrive there and know them by inhabiting them."

"Every ultimate fact is only the first of a new series. Every general law only a particular fact of some more general law presently to disclose itself. There is no outside, no inclosing wall, no circumference to us. The man finishes his story— how good! how final! how it puts a new face on all things! He fills the sky. Lo! on the other side rises also a man and draws a circle around the circle we had just pronounced the outline of the sphere."

LETTER TWO

An illustration of the "nuggets of gold" we may find, if we go deep enough into Being.

Dear Friend:

I AM glad I returned here in time to receive and answer your letter today. I thank you for the enclosed offering and more for your words of appreciation and the proof of earnestness in the questions you ask. You are a student "after my own heart" as you are going to sift the matter of understanding to the foundation, and I joy in such a correspondent. We will take the question you say perplexes you—"imaging supply." You say the body is a tangible presence so you can easily see how health can manifest therein; well, money is a tangible body through which wealth may manifest. You ask, can we by simply sitting down and imaging a million dollars, get it? I will refer you to Isaiah 30-7, also 55-9. Then Jeremiah 32-17 and 27; Hebrews 4-10—the whole chapter is helpful.

You may have had similar experiences to this: A lady once while working about her house idly hummed all day, "In the bosom of the lily, Christ was borne across the sea." At night she was presented with a beautiful white lily, greatly to her surprise and from a very unthought of source. You see she concentrated upon lily and so presented the mental picture, or image, to the conscious intelligent Law; and because she was not trying to, so did not intrude a single doubt, the Law had no opposition, so worked perfectly as *it would if she had seen herself receiving "a million."*

But let me assure you that to be idle personally does not mean idleness on all planes of Being, by any means. You know that *Being* is *three fold*. The inner, the most intense vibratory substance, Spirit, all knowing, all powerful: the outer, the material, plane; and the middle space, the plane of the "mediator" or conscious thought and will. So the inner does not act directly upon the outer, but because it is always intense activity presses upon the conscious plane as Desire, pushing and urging the conscious plane on to expression. So now, my dear, do you not see how and why we may be idle, or, rather, still on the outer plane? (I mean we who are awakened). For we are now supposed to be conscious of our oneness with the real or central self, and living and acting from that plane. It is the "region in man that is never ill" as Emerson says, and it is the region, too, where we "have received" that which we desire. This makes clear, does it not? That "desire is the thing itself," as Cady says.

It is the middle or conscious plane that has "had its back turned to the reality," so doubts and says "impossible" and that we must *labor* to grasp what we desire.

The middle plane says, "I am poor," like the old man who eked out a bare living plowing up a stony bit of ground for vegetables. One day his horse passed on and while digging a deep hole in which to bury him he turned up nuggets of gold. So if *we* go *deep* enough into Being, we find *that which we did not know existed.*

To illustrate again: The central real Self, One with all, is the dynamo; the middle or conscious plane is the directing power, and the outer plane may be compared to the wires and bulbs. Do I think it selfish to desire material things? Yes, I think it is Selfish or allowing the Self to manifest itself as all good to us, as it is ever trying to do, and what others say or think about it makes no difference to me. I am *honoring* Good to trust its providence in any and every way, "In *all* thy ways acknowledge me and I will direct thy paths." I believe in high ideals of attainment, the higher the better, but every victory over lesser affairs strengthens our faith and courage in undertaking greater ones, and I believe it is our duty to try to demonstrate harmonious environment, as that, as much as anything, conduces to peace of mind and admits of more time and freedom for spiritual growth and the working out of finally the highest ideals.

To experience lack is a "denial of God," as it is equivalent to saying, "here is a condition where Good is not," and very inconsistent with our affirmations of the "Omnipresence of God (Good)."

Another thought, and I am done for this time The ability to

demonstrate, proves that we have "first sought" and are entitled to things added.

It was ever so dear of you to typewrite those copies for me. If you think this has cleared away the fog that your questions indicated, and is worth your time, I would consider myself amply repaid if you will do the same with this letter. This would be an exchange of love for love, and indeed every transaction should be with love for a motive. We have, oh, so many opportunities to express a selfless love, and I believe when we come to consider all desire for the beautiful as only the craving of the soul for its own rightful estate, we will take a different viewpoint concerning the demonstrating of a more refined environment and see that one cannot be too selfish regarding its rights. I have put this deepest of occult truths as clearly as possible and it is the result of my own meditations and experience. The good old Bible is my authority and support for my theory, and is all one needs to study to perfect one's self spiritually. If you do not yet see clearly, I will gladly try to make clear anything that I have said that may seem abstract and impracticable.

Lovingly,

FRANCES LARIMER WARNER.

Nothing was ever brought into visibility without a concentrated effort of the mind, and to concentrate is to recognize, and to recognize is to acknowledge."

"All is yours, 'tis but by asking.

Ere you send your silent plea,

Heaven unlocks her richest treasure

For your waiting eyes to see.

All is yours when Faith upholds you,

Sets your wondrous spirit free:
For our mighty One has promised,

He your all in all will be."

LETTER THREE

How it is absolutely true that we may have our external life what we will; with an example of such demonstration.

Dear Friend:

HAVE just returned from a trip and found yours of the 2nd with several other letters, awaiting attention. Will reply to your letter as I read. You speak in the first place of "the spirit long bound," etc. I was left a widow at twenty-eight with an infant son, lost all I had in foolish speculation in California. My belief in lack, and want of a home, deprived me of every comfort until very recently I have demanded because of my divine right to all good, and have realized, not by constant affirmation, but by a method of my own, discovered after ten years of almost constant meditation, concentration, and experimenting with the Law. The results I freely give.

In reply to your question, well, I was "no longer young" and "unlucky." In fact, your portrayal of yourself fits my old self exactly. So take heart and never lose heart, as could you have known my old environment you would feel that you perhaps have less to overcome. Your letter touched me deeply, more so than any of the many received, as it pictured my old self so nearly, and I say to you that it is absolutely true that you *can* have your external life *what you will—yes, without* great time and concentration—and I am going to make the way clear and plain to you.

It is purely scientific that *"Out of the imaginations of the heart, cometh the issues of life,"* so even contrary to your reason, if necessary, never image, think, or voice a condition undesirable as the *first* step toward realization, but begin right now to see *vividly* your desires for a better environment and more congenial work *already fulfilled;* as the urge of life which presses upon the consciousness as desire, is *always* urge, and as a consequence *must be* followed with fulfillment. Jesus was very scientific when he said, "Believe that ye *have* received." When I discovered in lesser ways that I really had proven a mighty Law, I went deliberately to work to prove the ability of the Law to provide all that I demanded without the aid of my personal efforts or work. I was to all appearances without a home or the means to provide one, so I said, "This is my glorious opportunity to prove," and I first gave thanks for that, then every day I saw myself (vividly) in my home, at my desk, walking about the grounds, and as a matter of *research,* and *scientific test* as to the working out *in detail* of all of my mental picture, I saw myself jumping gaily into my automobile. This putting one's self at once into the actual environment desired is acceptance, or active faith. "Faith without works is dead," you know; a passive faith is never productive.

I did not once question as to *how* all this was to come about, as that was no concern of mine since I had been invited to prove the Spirit through Mal. 3-10. If we plant a seed in the ground we know that the sun will shine and the rain will water, and we leave it to the Law to bring about results. We do not see the process in nature, do we? Well, the desire you image is the seed, your occasional closing of the eyes in imagery is the sun, and your constant, though not anxious, expectancy is the rain and cultivation necessary to bring *absolutely sure results,* because relying upon Law. Of course, the ideal is the first requisite toward attainment. I had so limited myself that at first it was like pulling against some great force to even try to form an ideal higher than I had realized, so I just practiced forming ideals until I could form and hold easily the highest of which I could then conceive, so feel that I have broken the chain which bound me to limited conditions. It is better to take one thing at a time at first, and not a greater undertaking than that in which you can put your present faith.

Well, my dear, in less than one short year all that I imaged, and a great deal more,—as though for an added blessing for relying *wholly* upon Spirit for what Jesus had told me *was* mine,—came into my actual experience, and vastly more than possession is the joy of having proven to myself and others that all we need to do to realize all good is to study earnestly and faithfully, and then *practice* the teachings of our first great scientist, Jesus of Nazareth,

Faithfully yours,

FRANCES LARIMER WARNER.

"With each strong thought, with every earnest longing for aught thou deemest needful to thy soul, invisible vast forces are set thronging between thee and that goal. 'Tis only when some hidden weakness alters and changes thy desire, or makes it less, that this mysterious army ever falters or stops short of success. Thought is a magnet: And the longed-for pleasure, or boon, or aim, or object, is the steel: And its attainment hangs but on the measure of what thy soul can feel."

LETTER FOUR

A consideration of concentration and desire, and why there are no "have tos;" with a lesson in active faith.

Dear Friend:

YOUR beautiful and very appreciative letter, with thank offering enclosed, was duly received and I am so sorry to have been over a week in replying. While I have come to believe in an *everyday Christmas* rather than a one day Christmas, still just this season seems full of obligations that cannot be shifted all at once, as those unawakened are slow to understand. Will reply to your letters as I re-read them, and am glad you gave me your special stumbling stones.

So many are troubled about concentration, and I for one have given up trying. Just imagine the father of your flesh, kind, love itself, able to do all you ask of him, tender and near to you, and at the same time holding so aloof from you that you were compelled to enter the silence for hours at a time in order to fit yourself to dare to approach him in sack cloth and ashes. Spirit, Good, does not have to be approached in any such way. Just you make Good a living present reality and then be definite and tell Spirit just what you desire, and at the same time thank It for *always* granting.

Yes, Professor Northrup is right. We are *always* in touch with the hem of the garment and that's all we have to know. And this is why I realize through imagery, and I do not use words at all because I *know* that the urge of life which presses upon our consciousness as desire is *always* urge, and *must* be followed up with fulfillment, as steam in the boiler is followed up with *action* in the direction chosen by the engineer. Because *he* is sometimes *ignorant* of the *power he is using*, does not prove steam a fickle good. So when we misdirect the power within, we suffer, do we not? *Through* our ignorance in directing that power and never *for* our ignorance. I think it was our good Mrs. Militz who said that we were pressed upon by Spirit as the water presses the fish, "In it we live, move and have our being." To me Christ is *process* or *Law*, and Jesus taught that, for he said he did what wonders he performed by the use of Law. I think Rev. 12-10 makes it clear that Christ or Law is the *way* God operates through the universe. Now I wonder if I have made concentration and desire clear to you? If not, let me know and I will try again. You know by this time that I believe in a present help in time of trouble, one that does not have to be sought out through hours of concentration or *implored* in any way. When the ship seemed sinking with the disciples they "cried out" knowing help was right at hand, and so it ever is, only we save time by crying our thanks, for "to him who hath shall be given" so take whatever you want by *seeing desire fulfilled.*

As I read still further in your second letter, or rather last one, I am impelled, in reply to your query, "If desire is the thing itself, why did my desired occupation never come to me?" to repeat a story I have told before. Once upon a time, a man owning an old horse and stony little piece of ground from which he thought his only source of supply came through raising garden truck to sell, lost his main dependence, his faithful old horse, and while digging a deep hole in which to bury him, he turned up nugget after nugget of gold. Now, that is a parallel case with yours. Why didn't he spade up the gold before? Simply because he didn't know it was there. You had to learn, did you not? That the primal essence (desire) was your individual piece of ground, (pure substance,) to be molded into form by your conscious deliberate decision of what you desire. It makes no difference to It whether it forms itself into a hovel or mansion, congenial or uncongenial work, since we are not to be deprived of free moral agency, or choice.

But, oh, dear heart what do I read next from your letter so full of earnest desire to know? You say "ever since I had to drop my art study" and that "commercial life is so distasteful to me," and on top of that you say that, "while I *have* to remain in my present work, I should like to succeed in it." Well, did *Good* say you *had* to drop your art work? And did you ever yet see any one succeed in work uncongenial? And *do* you have to remain in it? I say no, no, *no!* Your very dissatisfaction is the revolt of a hungry soul for "something beautiful on which to thrive"; and can you imagine a human parent so cruel as to implant in an offspring a desire for an ideal work with no shadow of hope for its fulfillment? Away with such a heavenly father. Jesus said, "All that the Father hath is mine," and, "As I am, so are you"; so, all that the Father hath is *yours*, and mine, and everyone's.

Now, if art is your desire, why don't you begin right now to image yourself in your studio, either teaching a pupil or arranging your pictures or getting your "shingle" ready; think up what you are going to say on your studio sign, etc. Of course, do the work in hand while doing it, but at other times build your ideal in the astral world and it will take form in the outer world. This last from Lillian Whiting. The Truth I desire to emphasize is this: That the heart longing for one's ideal work must include its possibility. So, in reality, you did not have to drop your art work, as the urge that implanted the ideal contains also, as the acorn the tree, the means of attainment.

Every possession I now have came as the result of my active faith, and not through the work of my hands in uncongenial work, or even through the work of my brain. I began just taking God at His word and seeing myself in possession, since our first great scientist said that in order to have, we must believe that we had already received and give thanks accordingly. This may all seem abstract to you, because new, perhaps; but I assure you it is being demonstrated as the rule rather than the exception by many scientists who have dared to assert their spiritual birthright to know. Understanding is the price of power and is free to all who will worship at her shrine. "He that getteth wisdom loveth his own soul; he that keepeth understanding shall find good." Prov. 19-8.

Cordially yours in Truth,

FRANCES LARIMER WARNER.

Trust in thine own untried capacity as thou wouldest trust in God Himself. Thy soul is but an emanation from the whole. Thou dost not dream what forces lie in thee, vast and unfathomed as the grandest sea."

"Every trial is an opportunity in disguise; do not let it slip by unmastered. Boldly take away its mask, and you will be glad that you have this problem to solve. What was before looked upon with fear and trembling, will present brighter aspects to you; and you will be pleased with what you now account a misfortune."

LETTER FIVE

Some thoughts to bring freedom, and healing of the body.

YOURS of the 18th inst. is at hand, and in reply will say that we know that the desire to overcome is half the battle, and victory must be ours, as the same urge that is pressing on to perfection the purest flower that blooms, is pushing you on to the desired goal—and the more speedily, now that you are placing no barriers in the way. Oh, is it not glorious to learn at last that we are only suffering through our mistakes, not for them as we used in our ignorance to think, and that Good, like the sunshine, is always and eternally pressing towards us, urging itself upon us and finally urging so hard that we are compelled to awaken at last to the truth that we might have saved ourselves all of those hurts and bumps. But we no longer look back and mourn over lost time, as we know that the infant soul just emerged from the chrysalis of humanity is not subject to time, and it has all it can do in getting used to the new regime. The life that was almost a burden has become conscious of its Oneness with all Life; and joy, and the peace that passeth understanding, are now its portion, and it is content.

I can read, oh, so much, between the lines of your short letter, of the dead past, the struggle for freedom, and now the final overcoming through this wonderful revelation of Truth that has come to us who have ears to hear. For the two claims you ask relief from, although I am not now practicing healing of the body, here are some thoughts that will bring you freedom from them. You know that the root cause of nervousness is irritability, perhaps through heredity. You as a free soul never were nervous or irritable from any cause, for your inheritance is from and of the Spirit, perfect, changeless, pure, good. For the other; in this one presence there can be no loss of any kind. It is eternally recreating, restoring, healing, cleansing, purifying and energizing. Every fiber of your being is now vibrant with pure life which cannot be defiled, lost or turned from its course of perfection.

Since you gave me no permanent address I will not write a longer letter until I am sure that you receive this, as it has been some time since you wrote me.

Trusting that you will receive some light and comfort from what I have written you, and promising to hold you in mind to the Truth of your being, I am,

Faithfully yours in Truth,

FRANCES LARIMER WARNER

"If Joseph had not been Egypt's prisoner, he had never been Egypt's governor. The iron chains about his feet ushered in the golden chains about his neck."

"Flee from the goods which flee from thee: Seek nothing—Fortune seeketh thee: Nor scour the seas nor sift mankind, A poet or a friend to find; Behold, he watches at the door! Behold his shadow on the floor!"

LETTER SIX

A lesson in manifesting prosperity; how we may escape the experience realm.

Dear Friend:

IN my old thought I would have said, after reading your straightforward letter, how strange that we all seem to reach Truth through some form of suffering; but now I know that it is with us as with the butterfly, there is a struggle that is the birth pang of a new, free, and happier existence. A youth once watching the seemingly painful efforts of a butterfly emerging from the chrysalis, took his knife and, as he thought, helped it, and it emerged easily but with no colors. I can now look back to all material assistance as the knife which robbed me of Self-expression, and delayed my freedom many years.

You are wise indeed to seek the inner source of supply, as it is the fountain of all good besides, and "easily entreated." And now where shall I begin to help you to "manifest prosperity?" It is so very simple and easy, that it seems ridiculous that we have been so slow to discover. There are so many clear teachings in the most scientific of all books, the Bible, that now that we are beginning to discover that it is a scientific, rather than a religious book, we are comprehending and proving its teachings as never before. It is always helpful to read Lord, Law, since that which lords it over us is our Law and vice versa. So we are ruled by the Law until we discover that we, ourselves, make the law, and then we rule. This conscious intelligent Law is in ceaseless operation, and is wielded by thought, hence, "As a man thinketh, so is he"; and since even desultory thinking is creative and brings results, we have discovered that premeditated, orderly thinking for a purpose matures that purpose into fixed form, so that we may be absolutely sure of the result of our dynamic experiment.

There is a still higher form of the same creative energy which the ancients called the Law of Alchemy, where we rise into a realm where time is not a factor, and matter does not figure. Jesus did all of his demonstrating through his knowledge of this higher Law, and one of the deepest teachers I ever had, Mr. Arthur See of "The Higher Thought,'" taught that we could actually skip the experience realm and enter into instant realization. It was difficult for me at that time to comprehend, but since further research and personal experience as proof, I can endorse his teaching as perfectly rational and possible. Am I getting into too deep waters for you? I think not, for your letters show that you have been a student along these lines; but I will try to simplify as much as so deep a subject will permit.

You imply in your letter that prosperity is, since you ask me to help you to manifest it; well, thank Goodness it really is and I am sure I can make it clear to you. We will take steam for an example; it has both substance and power but lacks intelligence, so cannot be truthfully compared to the trinity of omnipower, omnipresence and omniscience, but here is where I hope to make my point clear, there is a substance and a Power that is Intelligence, and oh! do you not see and cannot you too exclaim, "My Lord (Law) and my God (Good)?" Then what? Well, simply this: translators tell us that God and Good are one and the same, then all good is God or Spirit solidified or made visible as steam into water. Now do you not see how we may escape the experience realm and comprehend something of the Law of Alchemy as the ancients called the Law of Spirit? If Good is omni (all) presence, and omni (all) power, and functions through its highest form, man, as omni-science (all knowledge) controlled by thinking, are you ever separate from that Presence which has the Power to form Itself through conscious knowledge, instantly, because of no opposing power, into your prosperity or any other form you may desire?

This may all seem abstract to you but it is very interesting to me to see in my replies to letters, how each one draws to himself that which he desires and must be ready for, or it would not be given to me to write each and every one a distinctly individual letter, and often of truths I had not myself clearly comprehended until replying to queries from students. So it must be that we desire because of the attraction of the object desired, as Cady says, and its pressure upon consciousness causes us to give expression in words to desire, not comprehending hitherto the true nature of desire and that the very cause of desire was the object of that desire trying to objectify itself into fixed form. So now we can clearly understand why we are told in Psalm 27 to "wait patiently and you shall have the desires of your heart." The Psalmist knew the nature of desire and that it was the effect of cause and that cause was the substance of the thing desired, hence he gave us this purely scientific statement, and nothing but our superficial interpretation of this wonderfully helpful and scientific book has delayed our freedom, for Truth does make free, and "Ye shall know the Truth."

You may have to study rather than read this letter as it is very difficult to put metaphysical truths in simple English, as it is an effort to make the unseen visible and only the spiritually awakened "have eyes to see."

Trusting that you will find the above helpful after careful study, I am

Yours in Faith,

FRANCES LARIMER WARNER.

*"Let no man pray that he know not sorrow, Let no soul ask to be free from pain,
For the gall of today is the sweet of tomorrow, And the moment's loss is the lifetime's gain.*

*Let no man shrink from the bitter tonics Of grief, and yearning, and need, and strife, For the rarest chords in the soul's harmonics,
Are found in the minor strains of life."*

LETTER SEVEN

Warning against dividing one's forces, and an example of how we may bring our desire to visibility.

Dear Friend:

To reply at once to your queries as to "whether one really can, without striving for it in the old hard way, attract all one desires of both spiritual and material blessings," and "would one have as great a sense of appreciation if attained without great personal effort?"

I am rather glad to have hacl these queries presented, as it recalls to my memory several instances of realization through faith alone, and in one instance I am very sure that the sense of appreciation was not diminished, but intensified a hundred fold, as in after years I derived many valuable lessons from it. I think that every proof of faith that one can have, encourages our trust in the Law of faith, so I will relate these experiences for your benefit. Will give this one of my own first, just as it occurred.

I was living in a village in Southern California about twelve miles from San Pedro, and went often with friends to the rocks below Point Fermin Light House, at low tide, to hunt for shells and moss. Every time I went some one of the party would be fortunate enough to find a particular shell that I thought very rare and beautiful, and which I was never able to find. Well, the last time I went to this place I determined to find one of these particular and much coveted shells, and said so in no half-hearted way, to the friend with us. We usually took a luncheon and spent the entire day searching for treasures that came in with every breaker. All day long we climbed and searched; whenever we found some rare trophy, calling to one another above the roar of the waters as they boomed under and around the immense rocks. Always before, I had searched for both moss and shells, always wishing for this shell but never with a determination both willed and expressed, to get it. This day I did not divide my forces by looking for moss and shells but concentrated all day long upon the shell. My friend called to me that it was time to start on our homeward drive as it would soon be dark. I consented reluctantly, as I had not secured the shell that I had fully determined to have before going home. We started up the long steep cliff and had gone about thirty feet when I said, "Oh, Miss H, I just must run back and take one more look," so I ran, half sliding, down the steep bank and straight out to the ocean where a great breaker had just deposited a pile of sea weed or kelp, and there, right at my feet, all dewy and glistening on the rock where it had just tumbled out of the wet sea-weed, was my beautiful shell. I fairly screamed with delight, of course, but was not so impressed with the deep significance of the incident at the time, as it was long years before I became a scientist. But now I love to recall it as a proof of the saying that "we have already received," and I firmly believe that the attractive force of desire started the object of my desire toward me, and my unwavering determination and concentration all day, brought it finally into visibility. And had I not obeyed "the still small voice" within and persevered until the last moment, I never would have known that my prayer (desire) was already granted. We are told, you know, in Psalm 27 to "wait, wait patiently on the Lord (Law)" and "you shall have the desires of your heart." Remember this, and that you may be giving up, as I came so near doing, just a moment before you might come into full realization. So wait patiently on the Law.

Another incident is this: A little girl came dancing up to my friend's carriage as she sat waiting before a store, and said, "Oh Mrs. D, see my new dime!" When my friend laughingly asked how she came by it, she answered, coming close to the carriage; "I will tell you because you will not laugh at me—whenever I count twenty white horses I find a right new dune." Think you this reward of a beautiful faith was more lightly esteemed than if earned by the "sweat of the brow?"

One more example as proof of the ability of Spirit to provide through other means than the natural, and I will bring this lengthy letter to a close. A dear little boy of four years used to go alone a short distance to his father's store. One morning he picked up a piece of money from the floor, near a seat at the counter. His childish faith led him to believe that he would find one like it every morning, so he went regularly every day, and as regularly picked up the money from the same spot on the floor. One day his mother said; "Fred, why do you go to the store every morning?" "Oh, to get my money!" The mother inquired into the matter enough to learn that he had found a piece of money for several mornings, but laughed and told him that he would find no more as someone "just happened" to lose some. The child's faith was destroyed and he picked up no more silver. The boy, now a man of forty or so, was one of my instructors in the beginning of my study of mental science, and he deplored the fact, as we all must do, that his mother was the one to destroy a faith that if encouraged would make life one song of gladness and enable each and every one to attain to the mark of their high calling. Faith is the secret of occult power but can become the rule of our every action, rather than the exception, and is the one thing above all to be attained.

Trusting that you may see clearly from these few examples the great importance of cultivating a child-like faith, I am,

Very sincerely yours,

FRANCES LARIMER WARNER.

"Philosophy, wisdom and liberty support each other; he who will not reason is a bigot; he who cannot, is a fool; and he who dares not, is a slave."

LETTER EIGHT

How "failure" is due to lack of understanding and not a lack in reality; and what may be accomplished by imagery.

Dear Friend:

YOUR letter is at hand with offering enclosed, for which I thank you. You certainly have great faith to still stand by your convictions of Truth, though finding yourself, after having studied twenty years, still unable to apply it to the financial problem. Still you know it is Truth and are going to persevere till you do prove the all-power and all-presence of the Good. I was a close student for nearly ten years before I was able to prove it my supply, as well as my health and happiness, but I knew the failure was because of a lack of understanding and not a lack in reality: so the first step was to declare very positively my perfect understanding of the law of supply. I have discovered, too, that one must be positive in their statements. Well, after claiming understanding this light came to me— that my faith was like yours, passive. Now a passive faith is never productive, no matter how perfectly we may comprehend the Law of the Spirit. We may fully understand the law of electricity but it would do us no good until we put it into action or practice; for instance, my rooms may be all fitted out complete for electric lights, but the law of electricity does not turn on the light for me; that is my part of the work to perform. "Without faith it is impossible to please Good," in other words, Good or Supply has gone just as far as it can.

I know that wealth is as spontaneous as sunshine, and just as we can shut out the sunshine, so we can and do shut but wealth by our failure to do or act. So what you need is an active faith. I too concentrated for two years or more on Emilie Cady's chapter on faith till I became firmly convinced that faith was the Law through which Spirit worked, and that nothing should be impossible to me when I thoroughly understood this law. Well, since faith was the law to be applied to the fulfillment of my desires, how was I to apply it? The Bible gave me the key to the secret of active faith, and here it is: "Out of the imaginations of the heart, cometh the issues of Life." This is a mighty occult secret known to the adepts for hundreds of years. They enter a state called Nirvana where, as in a trance, they hold steadily the vivid mental picture of the object they desire to manifest, and with them it manifests at once, seemingly from empty space. In our every-day achievements we know that we do first image everything we do. Well, just go a step further and do consciously or deliberately, purposely, what before you only did as a matter of habit. This is the whole secret of my demonstrations, and since it makes no difference to the Law what we desire, we may as well make our demands great as small.

How good it is to learn that we are only limited by our own ignorance and that we can honor the great Law-Giver as greatly by proving Him our supply, as well as our health. Finances are the last thing to yield with most people, because of the great race belief in lack; so we must deny vehemently its power over us, then polarize ourselves to the opposite condition, or wealth, by sitting twice a day for thirty minutes seeing ourselves a center of attraction for wealth, as rays from a sun, or image the substance in which we "live, move and have our being" as forming itself into the symbol of wealth (money). I do not mean that it will manifest then and there for you, but in this way you set up counter currents that will soon replace those that because of your passivity have manifested a condition you did not desire.

When I demanded a soul mate and a home, I put myself in a home by seeing myself about the house and grounds always with a companion. Every little detail imaged has worked out till I know from experience that it is just a matter of choosing what we will have. This putting one's self into the actual position desired, is acceptance, or active faith. We may affirm till doomsday and get no results, unless we at the same time, either consciously or sub-consciously see ourselves in possession. "Believe that ye have received" bears strongly upon this argument. That oft misinterpreted verse, St. Luke 18-22, "Sell all that thou hast," means a giving up of all personal or limited sense of ownership and becoming an universal owner—"deny thyself and follow me." Give up the personal and become the universal, hence "treasures in heaven" (Spiritual abundance). Please look up Isaiah 55-9 and 30-7.

Pardon business paper as it was all I had at hotel. Trusting that you will gain some light from the above on the problem of supply, I am, very cordially,

Yours in Truth,

FRANCES LARIMER WARNER.

*"No mortal has yet measured his full force.
It is a river rising in God's thought and emptying in the soul of man. Go back to the Source, and find divinity. Forget the narrow borders, and ignore the rocks and chasms which obstruct the way. Remember the beginning. Man may be and do the thing he wishes if he keeps that one thought dominant through night and day, and knows his strength is limitless because its fountainhead is God. That mighty stream shall bear upon its breast, like golden fleets, his hopes, his efforts and his purposes, to anchor in the harbor of success."*

LETTER NINE

How to build consciously the home and environment we desire, and overcome financial limitation.

Dear Friend:

SINCE you have had the benefit of both Mrs. Militz's and Mrs. Kohaus's instruction, I doubt if I can teach you anything that they have not, as they are both so fine. Mrs. Militz was my teacher ten years ago in Los Angeles. You say that they told you that you were advanced. Well, my dear, if that is so, why are you in mourning, as your stationery would indicate? We are now living in a realm where all tears are wiped away, are we not? and we see all experience as Good (God). Those who pass on are born into a new experience, and have not known death at all, any more than you do when you fall peacefully asleep at night and awaken in the morning. And they were ripe for that experience or it would not have come, and it will be such a very little time now till we attain to a consciousness of Oneness and then we shall not sense separation.

You ask for a thought that will be helpful in overcoming a belief in financial limitation. The following seems to cover all seeming lack: **"How can I lack any good since mind is causation and I can think as I please?"** But better to me is the actually putting one's self in the position desired. When I said to myself there is a soul affinity and a home for me somewhere, I just mentally took possession, which was active faith. "Faith without works is dead," you know, so I accepted of the gift of Good by seeing myself in possession. Can you not realize that "what is not true of God is not true of you?" Practice this affirmation every time you are tempted to think lack, and stand apart from yourself and see it and your environment as just an expression of your wrong or ignorant thinking; and because it is that and nothing more, know that by the same mental processes you can build consciously a more perfect temple and surroundings. And isn't it so helpful to know that all we have to do is to direct this mighty power within, as the engineer the steam, and it works out our mental pictures? The engineer does not worry, does he, as to how he is to move the great engine? He just knows there is a power at his command and all he has to do is to keep a steady heart, hand and brain, and guide the great power in the direction desired.

It is very helpful to meditate upon the "I Am." First, become as quiet as possible, then say silently "I Am," until you can feel the powerful vibrations it creates, and yourself one with it. Then picture your ideal or desire, while in realization of this power, and you will soon see affairs begin to change. Go with the stream, and consider every incident as a necessary step toward fulfillment, even though it seem the reverse; and praise the Good that it is manifesting the supply that always was, but waiting for you to make expression possible.

Yes, we receive as we give, so a thank offering is helpful to the giver, as he then taps universal supply, as substance itself is the reality of all wealth. We limit by withholding the symbol (money), as symbol and reality are one. Man only limits, Spirit never. Hold this thought for supply: "Since I am one with the only Presence, I cannot be separate from that which I desire."

Yes, the address you gave is sufficient, as our addresses are not so complicated as yours in London. Thanking you for your kind appreciation of the article in September and trusting that you will derive some help from the above, I am,

Cordially yours,

FRANCES LARIMER WARNER.

"Earth's crammed with heaven, and every common bush afire with God, but only he who sees takes off his shoes."

LETTER TEN

A story of how we may limit realization by sense of personal obligation: being a lesson in "letting go."

Dear Friend:

OUR beautiful letter with the abundant proof of appreciation was duly received, and it has never been so hard for me to accept of a thank offering. My first impulse was to return it as a gift to the two little boys, then the thought "to him who hath shall be given" came to me and I said; "She is tapping universal supply every time she gives so freely and I can repay her a thousand times better by seeing her always as a perfect channel for abundant supply," and you may be sure I shall do so.

It did my soul good to read in your letter of the glorious way in which you overcame your really serious trial, and emerged refined as pure silver, seeing the good only in it all. My chastening was not in a domestic way but through losing all I had, and having had no training as a business woman I became simply frantic with fear of the future, with a young son to provide for as well; and this reminds me to tell you how I disposed of all sense of personal obligation as to his education, etc., after having come (through many years of worry that amounted almost to insanity), to a knowledge of truth. I learned at last that he was God's son, not mine, heir to all there is, and that the father of his real self was able to provide for His own, and that I had no right to set up an opposing force in the shape of doubt and fear and actually rob my son of his true inheritance through my ignorant thinking. Thought habits gain such a hold upon one that it was very difficult to refrain from trying to do in a human way, but as often as I did I could see the harmful results.

Well, my dear, I managed to hold to enough faith to see him through three years of college, and good is constantly coming to him; so that for years his friends have said, "What a lucky boy you are!" I am perfectly sure, knowing the Law so well, that had I continued to limit him to the seeming little that I could do for him, he would have been deprived of the greater good that has come to him as God's son.' So do, for the good of your two little sons, let go of them and see how good will come to them from "here and there and everywhere" in ways that you could not conceive or provide. By letting go, I mean do not inflict your fear and doubt upon their future. You know Jesus said, "Let the little ones come unto me" and that is all that is required of us as to responsibility in their behalf. You know there are so many beautiful promises to the widow and the fatherless; put your whole faith in them, and as we are told to do in Psalm 27, "Wait, wait patiently on the Lord (Law) and you shall have the desires of your heart."

Thanking you for your love offering and knowing that all good is yours, only waiting for you to allow it to manifest through your perfect faith, I am lovingly yours,

FRANCES LARIMER WARNER.

"Serene I fold my hands and wait, nor care for wind, or tide, or sea; I rave no more "gainst time or fate, for lo! my own shall come to me. What matter if I stand alone? I wait with joy the coming years: My heart shall reap where it hath sown, and garner up its fruit of tears. The stars come nightly to the sky; the tidal wave unto the sea: Nor time, nor space, nor deep, nor high, can keep my own away from me."

LETTER ELEVEN

The danger of a too great sense of separateness; and how the companionship or love we crave, may be ours.

We are at home again and trying to entertain company and at the same time get caught up with neglected correspondence. I have taken my card out of the magazine as we expect to travel for a year or so and I did not like to feel that letters are delayed in reaching me, having to wait for a reply. And, too, have thought after due deliberation, that one's work should be found "at hand," and for a year or two at least am going to do what I can in a local way.

Do you not think that your realization of your "heart hunger" for companionship may be delayed because of your too great sense of separateness? "In Love we live, move and have our being." I am sure that in my case I first came into a realization of the omnipresence of Love, and silent companionship, and wondered when I heard people say that they were "lonely." I think if I were cast upon a desert island I could not feel that I were alone. I firmly believe that if you will cultivate this feeling of Oneness with all Life and all Love, that you will see the tendency to "lose your friends" disappear, and that you will attract through nonresistance the individual companion.

There is a deep reason for assuming this attitude. God (Good) is associated with the universe through Law and order. Then we must comply with that Law in order to reap the benefit of it, or rather we must not oppose it. It is the nature or Law of Being to give, so by nonresistance we intrude no opposing force and must realize our desires through compliance with the Law of Being. I think your great desire for true companionship has perhaps grown into anxiety, and anxiety is doubt, and doubt is the opposing force that prevents the fulfillment of your desires.

It is good to hear that you have found my few letters helpful, and trust that this may help you to see wherein lies your seeming failure to demonstrate your great desire. You, of course, received my card from Pierce thanking you for your enclosed offering? I am keeping the addresses of students and hope sometime to meet them all face to face. Lovingly yours in faith,

FRANCES LARIMER WARNER.

"Always with me, I can never stray beyond His tender care, For our God is omni-present, here and there and everywhere.
Always with me—Love so tender feels each trembling breath of prayer, For our God is ever listening and His love is everywhere.
Always with me! every burden His strong arm will help me bear, For our God is omni-present—with His children everywhere."
"I know not where His islands lift their fronded palms in air, I only know I cannot drift beyond His love and care."

LETTER TWELVE

In which we see that our every thought is creative, because impelled by the one creative life-urge; and are reminded that the word impossible, as Napoleon said, is "very bad form,"

Dear Friend:

YOURS of inst. at hand. I thank you for your kind wishes about the new home that certainly is the result of deliberate imaging. You say in your letter that it seems wonderful that one can actually create his every ideal through visualizing. It is only strange or wonderful because we have not gone back to Cause. The wireless is wonderful but not so wonderful to the inventor who knows it through experimenting and constant study into the elements that combine to express it.

Well, my dear, let us go to the Source or creative Cause as a first step toward understanding our own creative power. "In the beginning God (Spirit) breathed" and "Man became." So the spirit or breath is man, therefore there are not two or many lives, but One life. Spirit breathes, man becomes—it is a continuous process. Well, since spirit and life are one and my thought is impelled by the one life urge, then is it so strange that thought is creative? And is it not easy to see the meaning in "As a man thinketh, so is he," and in this "If I should draw to me my Breath, all would perish" and "The Father and I are One?" We are taught nothing more clearly in the bible than Oneness. Oh, if we could only bear this truth constantly in mind that "Of myself I can do nothing"—that Spirit working in me is the one creative cause now and always, we would not be so slow to understand why our every thought must be creative. "You shall be held accountable for every idle thought" —so if even idle desultory thought is creative what an advantage to know it, and to realize that we have absolute freedom of choice as to what we think. "Choose ye this day whom ye will serve." In other words, choose between healthy, happy, rich, contented, beautiful thoughts, or sick, miserable, poor, unhappy, ugly thoughts. Our lives are absolutely ours to make or to mar, and every father's son of us is just where we are by the use of this mighty infallible Law, not chance.

You ask if it is necessary to see your home in detail. No, I did not; for I knew if I presented the picture of my ideal home as a whole I should not have the care of details. I did see the cobblestone chimney and grate. Now I am writing this letter before the grate. When we come to know absolutely that our every thought is creative because impelled by the One creative Life urge, then our ideals manifest in much shorter time. And why? Because we then intrude no obstacles in the shape of doubts, etc., but forge right ahead with the one unwavering thought of victory because of the promise based upon Law that "Nothing shall be impossible to you." Napoleon said that the word impossible was very bad form, but I say, that to say impossible of the hope of attaining to any height is to "make God a liar" because of our unbelief in his promises of the reverse.

To take your questions in order: No, the home will not be slower, but quicker to manifest because of your leaving all details to the Law. "Acknowledge me in all thy ways, and I will direct thy paths"—which means to me that the mind that is able to give "above all that we ask or think" can attend to a harmonious whole better than I can. Just demand and see as a whole the perfect environment that belongs to an heir of Spirit, and hold to it without wavering, and I can promise you, because of proof of this Law, that you will realize your heart's desire.

Yes, I do think, if you have not yet had verbal instruction, it might help you to realize perhaps, and yet if you can but grasp and act upon what I have written in my several letters and study earnestly the Cady lessons, especially the chapter on faith, you cannot fail to realize. I had to laugh at your saying you are no longer young, and only thirty, but we know in reality that time is but a measure of growth not a measure of age, so one should be proud to have attained to years of unfoldment. That is the comforting way in which I look upon my fifty years of growth.

I really do believe that the "thorn" is proving a blessing in disguise, as you are taking exactly the correct view of its existence, and so will, I trust, declare your freedom from it by giving it up and trusting to the Good to provide another position. Remember the experience of Jehosophat who when he began to sing and praise, smote the

Ammonites. So begin to praise the Good for having already provided your ideal work, then study Psalm 27.

Sincerely trusting that this may prove clear enough to enable you to demonstrate your desire, I am most

cordially yours,

FRANCES LARIMER WARNER.

"Do the thing and you will have the power."

"Spirit when discovered to the consciousness of soul seeks to clothe itself harmoniously and so casts out all error. Spirit is distinct from matter, though not from energy. It is through energy and Law that God is associated with the Universe. According to Hermetic doctrine, Christ is not person but process, by which man becomes transmuted into spirit,"

LETTER THIRTEEN

In which we are shown that no one is exempt from the law that as we give, in just that measure is it "meted out to us again."

MY morning mail brings me about fourteen letters with stamps enclosed, asking for instruction, which I am more than glad to give freely since Truth is free, still I do believe that a laborer is worthy of his hire, as far as his time is concerned, and in feeling that we cannot afford to give value received for instruction, we withhold our own supply, and no one is exempt from the Law, that as we give freely in just that measure is it "meted out to us again." Gifts of money are not always necessary, but some proof of faith should be made in order to open the way for our own continuous supply. "To him who hath shall be given" corroborates my argument that to feel that we have an abundance from which to give, surely sets flowing our invisible supply.

I am glad you wrote me so clearly as to your difficulty, as it has enabled me to discern clearly the cause of your inharmony. Don't you see, my dear, that the science of letters and numbers that you have tried to abide by, is a natural not a spiritual science? We have left the realm of the natural and pinned all our faith to the spiritual, and you can no more abide in both at once than the electrician can use the law governing steam for his electrical appliances. Paul says: "He who is governed by spiritual law is not subject to natural law." Natural law governs nature, but spiritual law is that supreme power which overcomes the natural. So all of our trouble comes, I am sure, from our trying to serve both "God and mammon." We must rely wholly upon one or the other, if we would attain to peace and freedom. This is why the instructions you sent me had no interest for me beyond curiosity, for "I am ruler of the sphere, of the seven stars and the solar year," and am not governed by stars, numbers, letters or anything else in nature.

No, indeed, it does not prove a weakness to have written me, and I think as teachers we all have about the same experience. I appreciate your kind words and am so glad to know you, too, through your letters and all who write me. And isn't there a feeling of nearness among us all that we never knew or could know as natural beings? The natural to me is only the chrysalis, and an incident that we are done with as a ruler at least So let us lay hold upon the "dominion" with which we were created and turn no more as Paul says, in Gal. 4-9, the weak and beggarly elements." Hoping that this may help you to abide under the shadow of the Almighty, I am,

Lovingly yours in Faith,

FRANCES LARIMER WARNER.

How can I lack any good, since mind is causation and I can think as I please?"

"The power to create one's own self, to manifest as one chooses and as one pleases is a tremendous right and privilege."

LETTER FOURTEEN

Something about fourleaved clovers, and why we do not find them; with a lesson in recreating the physical body by mental forces.

Dear Friend:

INDEED, I can tell you "why some people find four leaf clovers and others cannot," when the clover all about is full of them. A few years ago I was spending the summer with a niece in Wisconsin in a dear little Arcadian village nearly half a century old. It was full of quaint old places and we took long strolls nearly every day. One day my niece began picking four leaved clovers till she had nearly a hand full. I had never been able to find one, and said positively, "I never find a four leaf clover"; and then began to reason the matter out, trying to square it by the truth that All is Law. I have repeatedly made the same positive statement that I could never find a four leaf clover. It is very clear to me now why my "eyes were holden that I could not see," even when the object of my search was right before me. The subjective part of my mind was simply obeying my positive statement that I never found them. What else could it do but act upon the statement? Since to listen to and obey the positive statements of the objective mind is its office and function, and it is a faithful servant, you may be sure. Hence, "You shall be held accountable for every idle word." So I began to reverse the statement and to say, "I can find four leaved clovers." It took nearly a whole day to switch the old current of lifetime belief, but before dark I had found several, and my eyes are no longer holden as far as finding four leaved clover is concerned.

But what about other good things we may as well have, as to do without? If you are in the habit of telling this faithful sentinel of your every thought, that you cannot possess the beautiful things of life, that life is hard, and you are ill, etc., you may bank on getting what you expect but you can have all of the joys and good things of life at exactly the same price. Just think joy and gladness, and peace and wealth, and the environment will soon tally with your persistent thinking. Matter is never self-acting but acted upon by thought.

And this brings me to your second query as to whether one can re-create and improve one's form by mental process. Again I can go right to my own experience as proof that, "Nothing is impossible to him who believes." My weight, now 140, was ninety-nine pounds, and I belonged, moreover, to "lean kine" so no one can attribute my increased normal weight and improved form to heredity. I can give you a great many references in the Bible relating to this only legitimate means of attaining our desires; for in John 10-1 we are told very plainly that to enter the door of attainment through artificial means makes one "a thief and a robber." I began using "oil of gladness" for a smooth skin, and to report Good to my senses to make my "bones fat"—Prov. 15-30. Simple, is it not? and "not bad to take." But do not think for a moment that you can attain this desire with a divided faith, for "I, thy Good, is a jealous God," and only responds to a desire for good that is felt with "all your heart and all your soul" (Deut. 11-13) and in Job 33-25 we are told that the flesh shall become "fresher than a child's and we shall return to the days of our youth;" and in Isaiah 65-20, "for the child shall die an hundred years old." Is not this worth trying for according to the Law of Life, which is the straight and narrow way that all may enter who are willing to pay the price of compliance with Law?

Trusting that your eyes may be no longer "holden," and that you may attain your heart's desire through right thinking, I am,

Cordially yours,

FRANCES LARIMER WARNER.

"Matter never moves unless acted upon by some force that is not itself. The body never moves, unless acted upon by some force that is not it. Know thyself, and then you will know that which eternally moves, forms and reforms all

things in the universe."

"There is but one active intelligence in all Being."

LETTER FIFTEEN

Showing the state of mind that must precede imagery, and the folly of shouldering responsibilities which do not belong to us; with a lesson in coaching one's faith in abundance.

Dear Friend:

YOUR letter, referring to my card in Unity, is at hand and will proceed to reply to your queries. You say that you have tried imaging and failed to materialize your desires. There is a state of mind that must precede my method of realizing through imagery, and that is an acknowledgment of the same great law working all the time. Paul says, "When thine eyes see thy teachers, then shall thy teachers be removed," meaning of course, that when we realize that we are where we are by law not chance, and that the law, therefore, is good, and we really can do as the Psalmist says,—"Delight ourselves in the Lord (Law)," Psalm 37-4— then and not till then shall we have the desires of our hearts. I was a scientist many years before I was able, though trying all the time, to see the full meaning of the above quotation, and just as soon as I began to apply it and really feel that "All is Good"—yes, even the most trying experiences—then the light of understanding dawned and I was able to guide desire and its results more to my liking. You are perfectly right in thinking that things were "being moved" by your efforts, and that your "reverses must be good" as they proved your ability to set so mighty a force in motion, and, since its modus operandi is always forward and upward, you know that relief must soon come, since there is no opposing force. But, oh, my dear, don't you see that you are shouldering a responsibility that does not belong to you at all? Such a list of troubles, and you are trying to carry them all, when in reality there is not a human responsibility or care in the world for any one.

Oh, these poor tired faces and brows full of wrinkles and fear-thought! And why? Simply because we are willfully turning our backs upon an ever-present help. Yes, we scientists are doing so, too. If I were you I would image myself as tying those tribulations in a bundle and pitching them into a pit so deep that I couldn't hear them strike bottom. I was once in a seemingly similar predicament, and when the temptation came to worry over it, I would mentally show my troubles to the door and out with a vengeance, and actually rid myself of many serious problems in that way. Paul says, "Ye are not your own." I used to laugh at that verse in my ignorance, and now I rejoice because I understand it. If the I in me is not me, who and what is it? It is the "Living God" of which I am as a temple through which the latent divinity within reaches consciousness of Oneness with the Whole, or at-onement. Then all of these worries and trials belong to It and you are really meddling, officious. My! how we used to correct our children for that error, never dreaming that we were doing the same, only in greater degree— yes, really interfering with another's concern. This is the reason we feel the hurt of bumping up against the Law, or "kicking against the pricks" as Paul puts it.

I will tell you one good way to coach your faith in abundance. Begin right now to use freely the means at hand, even if it is with an "Lord, help thou mine unbelief" feeling, and furthermore when you crave refreshment or anything that will add to your comfort or that of the husband you say is ill, get it, taking no thought for the morrow, debts, or any other old trouble. In this way you will switch the old current of fear-thought and invite the opposite state of consciousness, belief in abundance. When a girl, a family living in the same town with us were a great puzzle to me and every one. They were always happy-go-lucky, and while everyone knew they had no visible means of support, yet they always seemed to be able to dress well, travel, move among the wealthy and do everything they desired as far as money was concerned. I now know that although unconscious of it, they were at the time living in perfect harmony with the Law of supply.

Then why do not we who know, demonstrate better conditions? Just because we allow ourselves to be held in a vise-like grip by that old monster, Fear. And what does that imply? A firm belief in the absence of God, of course, else knowing that God, All Good, is omnipresent— all-presence—why should we fear, or believe for a moment in lack or limitation in any way? Would it not be wise, just here, to remember that "Thou shalt have no other Gods before me;" and heed the comforting assurance in this: "Draw near to me and I will draw near unto you, saith the Lord?" It is absolutely necessary, since Spirit works through Law, to put one's self in harmony with the Law in order to receive and make it possible for Spirit to give. You see my dear, that what you are and what you have, rests wholly with you. Then, knowing this, and that as a man thinketh so he is, we may feel absolutely sure of the results of our persistent thinking.

Trusting that you will find a new and helpful line of thought in the above, I am,

Lovingly yours in Truth,

FRANCES LARIMER WARNER.

Let nothing make thee sad or fretful Or too regretful,

Be still.

What God has ordered must be right— Then find in it thine own delight,

Thy will.

Why should'st thou fill today with sorrow About tomorrow,

My heart?

One watches all, with care most true, Doubt not that He will give thee, too, Thy part.

Only be steadfast, never waver, Nor seek earth's favor,

But rest.

Thou knowest what God's will must be For all His creatures—so, for thee— The best."

LETTER SIXTEEN

Definition of active faith, and an example of the psychological moment for demonstration.

YOUR letter, with several others, was received just as we were leaving home and I am doing them the best justice possible while on the wing, as am with my husband on a business trip throughout South Dakota; then we return to Faulkton to start on an overland trip of several hundred miles with horses, an outing we have always desired to take. We are also in search of our ideal home or place to build a permanent home. I may not always receive my mail promptly as can only have it forwarded to certain points. Am very glad, however, to have heard from you and will give you what light I can.

If you read my little article on the demonstration of supply, you know pretty well my method, visualizing one's self already in the position desired. This is acceptance or active faith. You know a passive faith is never productive—"Faith without works is dead," we are told. As the sun could shine no more for our asking, so Good can give no more for our asking. We have now our part to perform, which is simply acceptance. Your room may be supplied with all appliances for electric light, but it does not turn itself on for you, does it? Well, Good has gone just so far and could not, if it would, go a step farther; since it too works through Law. Nature abhors a vacuum—so does Spirit; and the moment you desire is the psychological moment for demonstration. For instance I was on the street in Chicago one very warm day and think I never desired a cool refreshing dish more in my life but had so limited myself for years by a belief in lack that I said to myself—"No, I have only a dime left and I must 'save' it." Then a great revulsion came over me and I just laughed and said "Oh! Oh! what an awful slam on an all-bountiful Father," and I walked into an elegant ice cream parlor and got what I desired, went right home, and took a letter from the mail box with money enclosed. I kept it up and from that time the Law has always responded to my active faith.

I was without a home for years and since the Law knows no great or small I decided that it could give me a home as easily as it could give me an ice cream soda. I began seeing myself in my home, would image myself about the house and grounds, and in fact in possession of all that heart could desire, and in less than a year it actualized into my outer environment— all that I imaged and more.

"Whatsoever ye desire, believe that you have received" is, based upon infallible science. "Blessed are the eyes that see the things that ye see" implies a real substance not seen by the spiritually blind. When a child asks money of the father of its flesh, he does not know where or how his father gets his wealth or how he is able to give him what he asks for and he does not question as to that, he just believes that his father is wise and abundantly able to give what he asks of him. We absolutely must become as a little child, trusting where we cannot see, and ask, or rather give thanks, for having already received; then act as though God meant what he said. "He who believeth not God, maketh him a liar."

Well, my dear, I have given you enough to think upon and to practice for a while, and for your encouragement I can tell you that I have known many to launch right out into an active trust and faith and their absolute faith has never once been betrayed. You know that money is only the symbol of wealth, and when we fear to use the symbol, we close for the time all avenues for the inflow of the real substance of wealth; but when we use freely the symbol, we also set free or flowing the real substance of supply. Meditate upon this, for it is true. Let me hear of your progress and remember always that time is not a factor in Spirit but Spirit is Itself the Is-ness of all desire, desire being the first touch of the object desired, as Miss Cady says. Her lesson on faith helped me greatly to understand the Law governing supply.

Lovingly yours,

FRANCES LARIMER WARNER.

*"I know not whence I came, I know not whither I go; But the fact stands clear that I am here in this
world of pleasure and woe. And out of the mist and murk, another truth shines plain— It is my power each day and hour to add to its joy
or its pain. The trouble, I think, with us all, is the lack of a high conceit. If each man thought he was sent to this spot to
make it a bit more sweet, How soon we could gladden the world, how easily right all wrong, If nobody shirked, and each one worked to help
his fellows along. Cease wondering why you came—stop looking for faults and flaws. Rise up today in your pride and say, 'I am part
of the First Great Cause! However full the world, there is room for an earnest man. It had need of me or I would not be—I am here to
strengthen the plan.'"*

LETTER SEVENTEEN

Showing how we may so bind ourselves up in our desires as to prevent their realization, and how even our physical condition responds undesirably to thoughts of limitation.

Dear Friend:

YOUR letter was duly received but have been away. Letters had accumulated and with other duties, such as building a home, etc., it has been an unusual time, so your letter with several others, has had to wait its turn.

I have just re-read your letter and am reminded of a restless bird beating its wings against its cage, and I am sure that "In quietness and confidence shall be your strength," Isaiah 30-15. Yes, my dear, I do think that we must evolve to this truth, but as Timothy 3-7 says, "It seems that we are ever learning and never able to come to the knowledge of the truth." My demonstrations were not made without long years of first seeking. You have set the standard for your happiness under the pale of natural law. Paul says, you know, that "He who is governed by Spiritual law is not subject to natural law," and so vice versa. This choosing to live within the spiritual is the proving of the truth of the saying that "He who loseth his life shall save it." In other words, we give up nothing and gain everything. Then why are we so very loath to do so? Simply because we have never tasted of the joys of Spirit, so have no knowledge of anything higher or more soul-satisfying than the natural affords. But thanks to the Law that allows us to reap the effect of our own mistakes, we finally "arrive" at a place where we demand freedom from ignorance and its consequent suffering, and are willing to become as a little child and learn of Spirit. To me the joy of attaining to a place financially where I had not been before, was as nothing compared to the joy of having been able to prove the Law as Malachi invites us to do, or rather the spirit through him, so the blessing is not in the material things added but in the actual knowledge of a Law that never can be taxed to the limit.

In the case of providing for the sister and mother, you may be depriving them of the privilege of proving the Law of supply for themselves, by carrying their burdens for them. You should not for one moment carry them from a sense of duty, as that is never a right motive for any work. If your gifts do not carry the love vibrations with them, they were better not made at all.

I can only advise you in this way about the lover—say this to him mentally: "I desire the Truth above all things, and for us both, Divine Justice rules in all the affairs of our lives." Write no conciliatory letters, but leave it wholly to this great adjuster and you will be gratified beyond measure. Divine Justice has opened prison doors and set the captive free when human law had failed utterly. It is easily entreated and full of mercy. In your case nonresistance is very essential. You will have to relax your hold upon all of these desires before you ever attain them. This sounds paradoxical, of course, but the ways of Spirit are directly opposed to those of nature. You see you are bound up in your desires and so you are binding your present condition fast and not even giving it a chance to wiggle loose; so let go, relax, say you don't care—and feel it. Just try for one week letting all of these worries alone and see if it is not in result like that of nature's sweet restorer, sleep.

You see, dear heart, that even nature demands that we be still, in order for her to get in her perfect work. Well, that is always the demand of spirit, and how little we heed it until we get a biff that "knocks us sensible" and we are still because we have to be, then we begin to wonder if there is really not some other way out and we find that there is and that we can be spared all future hard knocks, for, "Her ways are ways of pleasantness and all her paths are peace"— [Prov. 3-17]—and, [in Psalm 119-165,] "Great peace have they that love thy law and nothing shall offend them." This last wonderful promise to those who love the law, who are willing to really feel that all is good.

I will tell you a way to change the habit of your hair which you ask to be specially treated. You say you are economical and often miserly. Your hair has expressed your thought of limitation and so has not grown abundantly. Begin to give out freely, not grudgingly. When a child, you imbibed mentally the same thought from your home life which you say was hateful to you. Hatred, the bible tells us, is a "deadly poison," so at that time you unconsciously poisoned the fluids. That should now be corrected by strong thoughts of love. Stop supplementing this mistake of the past and begin to praise your hair for being so abundant and beautiful and let the Spirit heal.

You ask for my terms for instruction. Truth is free of course, but for my time only have been having one dollar each for individual letters. Trusting that you will faithfully apply the ideas given you through me and that you will thereby come into that peace which passeth understanding, I am,

Lovingly yours in faith,

FRANCES LARIMER WARNER.

"'God wills but ill, the doubter said, 'Lo, time doth evil only bear; Give me a sign his love to prove, His vaunted goodness to declare.' The poet paused by where a flower, a simple daisy starred the sod, And answered proof of love and power: 'Behold! behold a smile of God.'"

LETTER EIGHTEEN

Demonstration simply acknowledgment of what already is; an explanation of the futility of acting abundance and thinking limitation.

Dear Friend:

TO reply to your letter as I read: Yes, Paul says, "How shall we learn without a teacher," etc. But I am sure that Miss Cady means that there must come a time when we must rely wholly upon the within for light and guidance.

Your letter explains so clearly your position to me, and reveals in great measure one prolific source of failure to demonstrate. Like so many, many souls, you are constantly identifying yourself with the outer rather than the inner man. Oh, if we could only realize that demonstration means simply acknowledgment of that which already is. We do not have to do Spirit's work for it, as "It is finished," "That which was, is now, and that which is to be, hath already been." You probably have electric wires and fixtures in your rooms and all you have to do is to "Turn on the light." You could get no more light, or sooner, by worrying about the dynamo and wires leading to your rooms, or meddling with them in any way. That is all you have to do to realize wealth—"turn it on" by acknowledging it as a reality. You do have to do that, for "Without faith it is impossible to please God," and what does that mean? It means that God, Spirit, must have a means or channel through which to manifest. As the sun cannot shine into a dark cellar when shut out, so wealth cannot flow to us individually, when shut out by our doubts and fears, and belief of lack as the reality.

Oh, I am so desirous of making this clear to you, for I love my pupils and know them so well through their dear letters, and long to see them free from this great bugaboo, to me the greatest, perhaps because for so many years my strongest claim of error. Read the twenty-seventh Psalm over, and over, it tells us to ask, or claim, our desires, and then, "Wait patiently on the Law and we shall have the desires of our hearts." Are these wonderful promises all untrue? No, indeed, but we are not patient, but get in a hurry, and think that we must do something to help the Law along, and so frustrate and delay the manifestation which was perhaps just ready to come into our external realm. Please get Lillian Whiting's "World Beautiful:" it is so very clear in its teachings about the dual self. You tell me in your last letter of the exact amount of your bank account, and that of your husband's. For many years I have not known the amount of money in my purse, did not know whether my husband (to whom I was married two years ago) had fifty dollars or fifty thousand and did not care, for to know the amount of the symbol is to limit. Read 1st Chron., 21st Chap., and see the result of David's numbering Israel. We do not count our money to praise it for being so great, but to see how little there is, and just what we can "afford," is not that so? You say that you spend your money freely, and yet it is with a thought at the same time of a small bank account.

You speak of your Doctor. My dear, you cannot hope to prove the Spirit as wealth, while denying it as health. Paul says, "Let not him that wavereth expect anything of the Lord" (Law). We must "abide under the shadow of the Almighty" if we would hope for absolute freedom from all error.

I can see from what you say in your letter that you are striving hard to live a belief in abundance, but belief without absolute knowledge is apt to lead us into using freely that which we have in reality put a limitation upon, as you did in giving your bank account. You see your acting abundance, while admitting the small bank account, are conflicting, and set up two opposing currents which is the "wavering" that must expect nothing. It is your divine birthright to be joyously, perfectly happy, and in allowing your husband's discontent to depress you as you have done, a vibration is created that is also out of harmony with supply, and has a great deal to do with the failure to demonstrate the positions you both desire.

If you will persevere in holding the thought I gave you, to arouse your husband to the Truth, it will awaken him; but is very apt in reacting against his positive old thought to cause a disturbance that may seem to make matters worse for a time. Can you not organize a reading circle and begin with Hudson's Law of Psychic Phenomena? He would read it, as it is so logical and has been made a college text book. William

Walker Atkinson's books, too, are so pleasing to read, and would not antagonize him in the least, and would arouse his interest in this line of thought.

Trusting that this may clear away some of the mist that seems to obstruct your spiritual vision, I am very

cordially yours,

FRANCES LARIMER WARNER.

"All true work is done with reference to the ultimate good of the Whole."

"Never value anything as a producer of eternal peace except the wee small voice of thy soul; the divinity within thee is the only power that can lead to eternal bliss."

LETTER NINETEEN

How spirit forms itself according to our demands; and why we need not produce anything, but only come to our own.

Dear Friend:

YOURS of the 21st inst. is just received, and as have a little spare time, am glad to use it in replying, first thanking you for the love offering enclosed. Am so glad that you have found a "rose in place of a thorn." The seeming accident, too, may prove that "All is good," as it will bring the lesson to you of just how to deal with it and similar cases that may come up for you to heal and prove the Spirit. Your brother's body is no part of him, but the instrument he uses, so now and always declare for him that he never met with an accident.

A seeming miracle occurred not long ago in Chicago, when a lady was thrown from her carriage and several bones fractured. She was a scientist as were the friends with her, and they instantly declared that she was not thrown or injured, and the Spirit acting upon that quickly proved its wholeness through the flesh.

You don't know how gratified I am and how gratified your real self is, to have you attribute every sign to its working, and the more you acknowledge it the more help you will receive. You say you find it difficult to make your visions seem more than dreams, and to appear possible as realities. It is the outer life that is the dream, and the vision does not have to become real as it cannot become that which it already is. Your ideal life is like a silver vase, always pure silver, but tarnished with false impressions, so all we have to do is to remove the tarnish by affirming, and seeing, the bright shining reality. So do you not see that you are not to produce something, only come to your own? Remember

"Whatsoever you desire" is already yours and "Nothing shall be impossible to you." Yes, at once, as you ask in your letter. You know that time is not a factor in Spirit—only a measure of man's growth, not of age or limitation of what we desire. The enclosed little picture may help you to realize, as it is a photo of one picture I held in mind when demonstrating a home, not a particular home or companion, but my own, and had it not already existed in Spirit I could not possibly have realized it.

Now read this carefully and often: Spirit is substance which forms itself according to your demands, and must have a pattern from which to work. A pan of dough is as willing to be formed into bread as biscuit. It makes as little difference to Spirit what we demand. "I am with you, as ye have spoken" and just know when you look at this picture of myself and husband that the reality always was, but only came into my consciousness when I demanded it. This is all for now, only I must tell you that the rest of my mental picture is only now looming into our outer horizon, the more perfect home with beautiful lawns on sunny slope. Will tell you all about it next time, and why it was slower in manifesting. Trusting that this may help you to a realization of your own, I am,

Faithfully yours,

FRANCES LARIMER WARNER.

"I know that my welfare is dear to the heart of being, and that I cannot escape from my Good." "It is the one Formless Simple of the Universe. Eternal and Omnipotent, that forms all that is— it is in, back, through and beyond all we see and know—it forms and sustains all that is combined and complex. We are all that."

"THE WORD WAS GOD."

The vast importance of realizing the true nature of "The Word" grows upon me daily, until I am led to try at least to express what, to my understanding, is the meaning of the above quotation, and others I will cite, concerning the "Word," which imply a power vested in words of which many have never dreamed. Ignorance of the great dynamic power we are constantly wielding is the sole cause of all suffering, without a single exception.

In the above quotation the word POWER may be substituted in place of God.

In John, 6:63, we are told that "words" are "Spirit," and that they are "Life." We are not confined, however, to Biblical teachings for abundant proof of the dynamic power of WORDS. We know from a material standpoint that words are alive; from the fact that they are the very expression of life, and but for Life there could be no words at all. So Life and Words are one—since to live is to think— and words are but thoughts made audible. Then, since life is God, and words are Life (or alive), we can understand, perhaps, as never before, just what Paul meant when he said, "It is a fearful thing to fall into the hands of the Living God;" and that "The word was the seed;" and that "God giveth to every seed its own body," etc. Oh! is it not clear that the Word is an ACTUAL LIVING SEED! and therefore, since law is as exact in the Spiritual as in the Natural realm, must bring forth after its own kind? Many of us have proven that it is truly "a fearful thing to fall into the hands of the living God," since we have been ignorant of the power of our words and have not known that we really should be "held accountable for every idle word," or be "condemned or justified according to our words" (as the nature of the word might be), from the very nature of words, because they EVERY ONE ARE LIVING,

GROWING THINGS; and so we have wondered why God, who is All-Good—always Love—should seem to send or permit some of the very trying, and even "fearful" experiences in our lives.

And right here I wish to give positive evidence of the power of the word in one case, where it did indeed prove "a fearful thing to fall into the hands of the 'Living God' or 'Word.' "While my son was attending Woodstock College in Canada, he was invited to dine one Christmas with a family in a suburban town. While at dinner the hostess suddenly exclaimed, "Oh, someone will be killed, for there are thirteen of us at the table!" In just two weeks she was killed by an electric car which collided with her carriage. Who can attribute that experience to accident, when we know that "I will be with you, as ye have spoken of and that there are countless statements in both the Old and New Testaments (or testimony) given us by those who knew whereof they spoke, because of experience and proof of this mighty law?

So let us remember that according to our words it will be unto us, and that a feeling of "fear" in those words is "perverted faith." Henry Wood says that Faith has both substance and momentum. So by our fears we actually set in motion a force which brings about the thing we feared. Job said, "The things I feared came upon me." Then it behooves us to speak ONLY the words of which we desire to reap the result, and, as Paul says in Phillippians, 4:8, "Finally, brethren, whatsoever things are true, whatsoever things are honest, whatsoever things are just, whatsoever things are lovely, whatsoever things are of good repute; if there be any virtue, and if there be any praise, think on these things," and we may add, "Hereon hang the Law and the Prophets."

"THE INVISIBLE RESOURCE."

Tried and Proven

"Blessed are they that have not seen, and yet have believed."
John 20-29.

In reading the August number of Unity, I ran across this item "We need a pipe organ in our auditorium; will some of our good friends please suggest an easy way to get one?" Indeed, I for one, can tell you of a never-failing way, having proven its efficacy many, many times. My present home, perfect soul companion, a sparkling ring on my finger, an automobile, and all of the good things of life are crowding themselves into this present year of my life, as the result of the persistent use of Spiritual Law.

In the first place, you do not have to "get" the organ. In Ecclesiastes 3-5 we are told, "that which hath been is now, and that which is to be hath already been." So in the Substance of all things your organ is now, and there is an "easy way" to cause it to manifest. A friend of mine desired a piano to place in the music room of a new house, but their home having cost more than they expected, money for a piano did not seem to be on hand, though in substance the piano was, as she proved in a few weeks. She began proving the creativeness of mind by never allowing a table, chair, or anything else to stand where the piano was to manifest itself, and never entered the room without seeing vividly the expression of a piano there. The time of manifestation, I have discovered, depends a great deal on the constant and vivid imaging of the thing desired, and I know from almost daily proof of this mighty never-failing Law, that there is not an air castle too great to see literally fulfilled. In Mr. Fillmore's article on "The Invisible Resource," second paragraph, he proves that the appearance of objects we see are only one side of them, and that their reality or ISNESS, is forever on the unseen side.

Many people wearing glasses, see objects that without glasses do not exist to them at all, nevertheless they are there to others who have more perfect vision.

Oh, why cannot we see that it is only because of imperfect spiritual vision that the unseen appears so unreal? but, thanks to this great truth that is gradually dawning upon us, we who are daily proving, are believing, "not having seen" only as we trace effect back to cause. It is so very interesting to watch the intricate working of this great mysterious law, and there are so many who stumble along with their whole interest absorbed in the external, that I would like to give just one of many experiences in watching the effects of deliberate imaging of an object in view, proving truly that it is out of the imaginations of the heart that the issues of life come.

White and green are my astral colors, so even when all the dollars I possessed were found "rolling up hill," I determined to have a ring set with green and white stones, or diamonds and emeralds. Every day I closed my eyes for a few moments and saw vividly the ring on my finger, and would image myself turning it on my finger and admiring it. Right away I had this proof that I had set the law at work; every time I boarded a street car, ladies wearing such rings would sit near me, even when there were other vacant seats. If I went shopping, I found myself at counters near people with such a ring on; if I went for a soda, I was attracted to a table where ladies sat wearing diamonds and emeralds. This meant to me that the good old law was doing its best to draw such a ring and me together, and it only needed my steady, understanding faith to finally enable it to place the ring on my finger; which it did as a gift in less than a year. At the time I began to demonstrate it, I did not know of the existence of the giver. The joy of possession, however, was swallowed up in the greater joy of having once more proven the truth of verse 13, Chapter 14, of John, "And whatsoever ye shall ask in my name, that will I do that the Father may be glorified in the Son." Indeed, how else can we glorify the Good, or in what other way can it manifest to us Its self, All Good, except through this one "straight white line" of4 our understanding faith and intelligent co-operation. One's highest ideals may be so easily realized through the knowledge and right use of this wonderful law, that no one can afford to remain in ignorance of so great a boon. It is not surprising that our first great teacher gave us as the most important of all duties the seeking first the knowledge of this realm, or Law, in such ceaseless operation, holding us accountable for every idle thought, since thought is its only modus operandi.

"Man's extremity is God's opportunity," so since this need or desire for a pipe organ is presented, why cannot we join in a circle like unto that which encircled the walls of Jericho, and cause this seeming lack to disappear as did the wall? The silent hour at 9 P. M. would be a capital time. The Spirit through Mal. 3-10 begs us to prove it, and is ever waiting and longing to prove itself the substance of all good to us. We as scientists should never lose an opportunity to co-operate with it. Let us send up a heart-felt, "We thank thee, Father, that thou hast heard us, and we know that thou hearest us always."

AN ELUCIDATION.

> "In all thy ways acknowledge Him and He shall direct thy paths."—
> Proverbs, 3-6.

Superficial interpretation of my article in September Unity seems to demand elucidation. To desire a piece of money for tribute, a pipe organ, loaves, fishes, a ring or any other material possession simply for the sake of selfish enjoyment would seem childish in the extreme, and to be able to demonstrate for that end alone would be impossible, since the time and depth of research required to enable one to really demonstrate would, as a natural corollary, compel the highest ideals.

To reverse an old saw, this seems to be a case where the means may justify the end, and the means was the one and only absorbing theme in my mind and to those who have looked no deeper than the "things added" there is no lesson. Satisfaction never has been and never will be realized through sense gratification alone.

To elucidate still further, diamonds and emeralds only typify to me pure substance and eternal youth. As the walls of my rooms are hung with inspiring helpful texts, so the ring is a text and a constant "evidence of things not seen;" and just as I love my Bible because it is revealing the "deep things of God" to me, so I love the ring, not as a bauble, but because it has brought me "face to face with Good (God)" and as one may reach the soul of a hungry man by first giving him food for the natural man, so I find easy access to souls hungering for Truth by first inviting them to ride in the "demonstrated automobile," so proving it a Spiritual good.

However, considering demonstration from a purely material viewpoint and so following the advice of the above quotation, if by so doing we could open instantly and easily a door swollen by moisture or straighten a tangled string that was consuming otherwise valuable time, would we not by ignoring such power, deprive ourselves of a very great privilege? There is scarcely an hour in the day that I do not find an opportunity to prove the Law, and to It there is no great or small. Electricity was no less a power expressed through its first crude form. To interpret Mathew 25-21, we first coach our faith in a few, or little things if you please, before we can possibly "rule over many things."

And, by the way, my attention is just attracted to the fact that demonstration all through the Bible relates to things, probably because we were, and many still are, in the Thomas stage of evolution where the tangible though no less spiritual proof is more helpful.

Complying with several requests to give more of my personal experience in proving the Law, will give one which left no room whatever for doubt of an ever-present help in time of trouble. Some time ago while on State Street, Chicago, at Christmas time, it became almost a struggle for life to make any headway through the dense crowds and I began to wish myself at home, when this Bible verse seemed spoken to me: "I will go before thee and make the crooked places straight." I looked instantly for the fulfillment of the promise. Suddenly many were attracted to store windows, others across the street and like the parting of the waters the human sea was divided and my path was indeed made straight throughout the entire day. I involuntarily exclaimed "wonderful," and then I knew why it was said—"And His name shall be called Wonderful:'

In closing, Rev. 2-7 comes to me, where so much is promised to him who "overcometh." Some are in seeming bondage to one error, some to another and who can say that to have overcome that fear and belief that was to him the greatest bondage, is not the victory over self counted in Revelations as greater than to have taken a city, and is he not entitled in some degree to enter into the "joy of the Law" (demonstration)?

TESTIMONIAL

"Mrs. Frances Larimer:

During the time that I was studying with Mrs. Larimer*, I was cured of chronic tonsilitis, constipation, and general debility; also I came into a full knowledge of my oneness with the Infinite, and a strong abiding knowledge that there was nothing to fear save my own thoughts. I now feel myself to be on the highroad to eternal success and happiness, and I attribute it to the faithful teaching that I received from her.

"Anna Louise Ambrose"

(now Mrs. Edgar Wallace Cenable). 135 S. Griffin Ave., Los Angeles, California.

*Now Mrs. Frances Larimer Warner.

To those who find these letters helpful and desire individual letters of instruction as to the overcoming of any seeming inharmony, I will gladly write personal letters, giving them the benefit of my years of earnest research and experience in proving the infallible Law of Supply.

As compensation for my time only, in writing lengthy letters of instruction, and as protection from those not thoroughly in earnest, a charge of one dollar is made.

FRANCES LARIMER WARNER, Philip, South Dakota.

You might also like:

The Power of Awareness

ISBN: 1479303968
ISBN-13: 978-1479303960

The Game of Life and How to Play it

ISBN-13: 978-1479355709
ISBN-10: 1479355704

How to Get What You Want

ISBN-13: 978-1480069985

ISBN-10: 1480069981

How the Mind Works

ISBN-13: 978-1479385997
ISBN-10: 1479385999

Made in United States
Orlando, FL
02 November 2023

38510306R00048